FUNNY CATS

FUNNY CATS

An Hachette UK Company
www.hachette.co.uk

Summersdale Publishers Ltd
Part of Octopus Publishing Group Limited
Carmelite House
50 Victoria Embankment
LONDON
EC4Y 0DZ
UK

www.summersdale.com

Printed and bound in China

ISBN: 978-1-80007-436-1

Substantial discounts on bulk quantities of Summersdale books are available to corporations, professional associations and other organizations. For details contact general enquiries: telephone: +44 (0) 1243 771107 or email: enquiries@summersdale.com.

FUNNY

CATS

CHARLIE
ELLIS

If I fits,
I sits...

summersdale

ONE SMALL STEP FOR CAT, ONE GIANT LEAP FOR CATKIND

HE'S BEHIND ME, ISN'T HE?

WHEN THE CATNIP HITS JUST RIGHT

DAY 33:
MY COLLEAGUES
STILL HAVE
NO IDEA THAT
I'M A CAT

HOW AM I SUPPOSED TO LIVE LAUGH LOVE IN THESE CONDITIONS?

WHEN YOU'VE GOTTA EAT YOUR VEGETABLES BEFORE YOU CAN HAVE DESSERT

WHEN YOU MANIFEST THAT YOU'RE GOING TO HAVE A GOOD DAY

I'LL TAKE MY MILK SHAKEN, NOT STIRRED

SURE, EVERYONE HAS A RIGHT TO THEIR OWN OPINION... IT'S JUST A SHAME YOURS IS WRONG

WHEN YOUR CRUSH WALKS INTO THE ROOM

BEFORE FOOD...

... AFTER FOOD

THE SWEET
POST-SHOWER
SIT-DOWN

100 PAGES IN AND I STILL DON'T KNOW HOW TO KILL A MOCKINGBIRD

WHEN YOU'RE NOT ALLOWED
TO TOUCH THE TREATS
UNTIL CHRISTMAS DAY

ACCORDING TO MY CALCULATIONS, IT'S IMPOSSIBLE FOR ME NOT TO BE A BADASS

FELT CUTE —
MIGHT DELETE LATER

WHEN YOU
KNOW WHAT
V-E-T
SPELLS

BROTHER!
HELP ME!

**THE WORLD IS MY KINGDOM
AND THIS IS MY CASTLE**

NO, DON'T OPEN THE DOOR! I SAID

DON'T OPEN THE DOOR!

**WHEN YOU'RE AT A RESTAURANT
WAITING FOR THE WAITER TO
SPRINKLE CHEESE ON YOUR DISH**

I USED TO BE WORSHIPPED AS A GOD

HAVE A CHILD, THEY SAID... IT WILL BE FUN, THEY SAID

FRIEND: WHY DON'T YOU JUST CALL THEM?

ME:

I COULD EXPLAIN, BUT I WOULD RATHER NOT

POV: YOU ARE
THE LAST COOKIE
IN THE PACKET

... MY BRAIN AT 3 A.M.

WHEN YOU OVERHEAR SOME DRAMA UNFOLDING

WHEN YOU ACCIDENTALLY ZONED OUT AND HAVE TO PRETEND YOU KNOW WHAT'S GOING ON

FRIDAY NIGHT...

... SATURDAY MORNING

LOOK, IT'S WORKING FINE –
YOU'RE JUST ON MUTE

11 MISSED CALLS

FROM MUM

OH MY GOD, I'M GORGEOUS

I'M FINE — THIS IS
JUST MY FACE

"THERE'S CAKE
IN THE KITCHEN"

WHEN IT'S BEEN A LONG WEEK
AND IT'S ONLY TUESDAY

I AM A FIERCE AND POWERFUL BEING. FEAR ME!

THEM: WE NEED TO TALK

ME:

MAYBE LIFE ISN'T ABOUT FINDING THE COMFIEST SPOT — MAYBE LIFE IS ABOUT FINDING COMFORT WITHIN MYSELF

WHEN A CUSTOMER WALKS IN TWO MINUTES BEFORE CLOSING TIME

SOMETIMES I LIKE TO PRETEND I'M A LITTLE LOAF OF BREAD

LOOK INTO MY EYES AND REVEAL
YOUR DARKEST SECRETS

AN IMPORTANT PART OF GETTING RIPPED IS THE POST-WORKOUT WARM-DOWN

WHEN YOUR ALARM
HASN'T GONE
OFF YET BUT THE
AMOUNT OF SLEEP
YOU'RE GETTING
SEEMS SUSPICIOUS

THEM: TELL US A FUN FACT ABOUT YOURSELF

ME:

WHEN YOUR NEW HOUSEMATE TURNS OUT TO BE A DOG

DO THEY NOT KNOW I'M A HOUSE CAT?

IF YOUR NAME'S
NOT ON THE LIST,
YOU'RE NOT
COMING THROUGH
THE CAT FLAP

IMAGE CREDITS

Have you enjoyed this book? If so, find us on Facebook at **Summersdale Publishers**, on Twitter at **@Summersdale** and on Instagram at **@summersdalebooks** and get in touch. We'd love to hear from you!

www.summersdale.com